Let's Do Lunch!

Written by
Kids Cooking Club®

Illustrated by
Yancey Labat

Scholastic Inc.

New York   Toronto   London   Auckland   Sydney   Mexico City   New Delhi   Hong Kong   Buenos Aires

Designed by Peggy Gardner

ISBN 0-439-83224-1

12 11 10 9 8 7 6 5 4 3 2 1   6 7 8 9 10/0

Printed in China.

First Scholastic printing, April 2006

We hear grownups use the popular phrase, *"Let's Do Lunch!"* when they want to get together during the day with someone special. Well that's because lunch is a special time of day when lunch tables at school are bustling with excitement and you're wondering what's in your lunch bag. Now you can help make lunch even more fun by creating and packing your own lunch! We hope our recipes will:

♦ Spice up your lunch (Taco Salad Ole' Ole')

♦ Have you gobble each bite (We're Talking Turkey Salad Pita)

♦ Put a smile on your face (Happy Face Soup)

♦ Make you zoom back for more (Racecar Sandwiches)

So, yes, let's do lunch together and let's start right now!

The Lunch Kitchen Rules

◆ **Read completely:** read recipes all the way through before starting. Several recipes require extra time for ingredients to marinate, set, or refrigerate.

◆ **Dress right:** wear an apron, short sleeves, and tie back long hair.

◆ **Start clean:** wash hands, start with clean tools and work area.

◆ **Be prepared:** get out all necessary ingredients and tools before starting.

◆ **Clean up:** put things away as you finish with them.

◆ **Be safe:** know where and how to use the fire extinguisher in your kitchen.

◆ **Have fun:** but don't play roughhouse in the kitchen.

◆ **Be supervised:** have an adult with you at all times in the kitchen. Grown-up supervision is a MUST when using the stove, oven, microwave, appliances, apple slicer, vegetable peelers, cheese graters, and knives.

NOTE TO GROWN-UPS:

All of the recipes in this book are designed for adult supervision **at all times**. Kids should **never** be left alone in the kitchen. There are many steps that grown-ups need to handle or supervise including, but are not limited to, stove, microwave, and oven safety; handling hot pans; working with sharp knives; operating appliances; overseeing kids using the oven and stove; and ensuring that the oven and stove are turned off after use.

 We have placed this icon next to those steps that will require your help.

PLAN AHEAD!

Please note that several recipes require extra time (hours or overnight) for ingredients to marinate, set, or refrigerate. Plan accordingly so kids don't get discouraged once they start a recipe and cannot finish it right then.

PLAN AHEAD! We have placed this icon next to those recipes.

The Lunch Kitchen Things You'll Need

Apple slicer: used to core and slice apples.

Can Opener: ask grownups help when using.

Colander: used to drain liquid from various ingredients.

Cutting board: have a good one ready. There is lots to chop.

Foil or plastic wrap: use to tightly wrap sandwiches you are packing for lunch.

Insulated Thermos or food jars: good for drinks, salads, and soups. Can keep items cold or hot.

Lunch box or sturdy lunch bag: personalize yours and be sure to include ice packs when needed to keep items cool.*

Measuring cups and spoons: you always need these when you cook.

*Freeze a juice box or bag to use as an ice pack and it should thaw by lunchtime.

Mixing bowls: have several sizes ready.

Plastic storage containers with lids: great for salads, sandwiches, dips, and snacks.

Plastic serving ware: have forks, spoons, and knives ready to pack in lunches when needed.

Plastic zipper lock bags: large ones are good to marinate and crush items.

Popsicle mold: great for the many Popsicle recipes inside.

Soup pot: for soups, chili, and Sloppy Joes.

Vegetable peeler: for veggies and potatoes.

Wooden Skewers: for satés.

Some Lunch Words You'll Need to Know

Canapé: a thin piece of bread with cheese, meat, or other spread. Served as an appetizer or at teatime.

Chunked: cut into about $\frac{1}{2}$ to 1-inch squares.

Diced: cut into small, even-sized pieces.

Divided: when an ingredient is used more than once in a recipe.

Grated: to rub cheese, fruit, or vegetables on a box grater to create fine particles.

Mince: cut food into very fine, small pieces.

Nosh and nibbles: snack or light meal.

Saté: strips of marinated meat, poultry, or seafood grilled on skewers.

Sauté: to cook on a stove in a small amount of oil.

Shred: cut into long slivers or slender pieces.

Chunky Fruit Salad with Zesty Dressing

This salad is so refreshing! Chill overnight in a Thermos and pack it in your lunchbox.

INGREDIENTS FOR SALAD:

- 3 apples, chunked
- 3 pears, chunked
- ½ small watermelon, chunked
- ½ honeydew, chunked
- 2 oranges broken into segments, chunked
- 1 cup fresh blueberries, raspberries, or strawberries

INGREDIENTS FOR DRESSING:

- 1 banana
- 1 cup plain yogurt
- 2 tablespoons brown sugar
- 2 tablespoons honey
- 2 tablespoon poppy seeds

TOOLS:

- Apple slicer
- Cutting board
- Knife
- Large serving bowl
- Blender

SERVES 6

Steps:

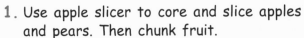

1. Use apple slicer to core and slice apples and pears. Then chunk fruit.

2. Chunk watermelon, honeydew, and oranges. Rinse fresh berries and mix all the fruit together in a serving bowl.

3. In a blender, combine bananas, yogurt, brown sugar, honey, and poppy seeds. Drizzle over fruit and let chill before serving.

Taco Salad Olé, Olé

A double olé goes out to this well-seasoned salad!

Tools:

- Skillet
- Cutting board
- Knife
- Large spoon
- Colander
- Mixing bowl
- Can opener
- 4 serving plates

Serves 4

Ingredients:

- 1 tablespoon oil
- 1 red onion, diced and divided
- 1 pound ground beef
- 2 tablespoons chili powder
- 2 tablespoons paprika
- 2 teaspoons garlic powder
- 1 teaspoon salt
- 1 red bell pepper, seeded and diced
- 1 14-ounce can black beans, rinsed and drained
- 2 cups corn kernels, drained
- 2 tablespoons lime juice
- 2 tablespoons olive oil
- Salt and pepper to taste
- 1 bag tortilla or corn chips
- 2 cups sharp cheddar cheese, grated
- Head of Romaine lettuce, shredded
- Optional garnish: fresh salsa and chopped cilantro, sour cream, guacamole

STEPS:

1. **Make the seasoned meat.** Heat oil in skillet over medium-high heat and add ½ of the diced red onions. Sauté for 2 minutes, then add ground meat, chili powder, paprika, garlic powder, and salt. Cook until meat is browned, about 5 minutes. Then drain in colander.

2. **Make the black bean and corn salad.** Put prepared red bell pepper and remaining diced red onions in mixing bowl. Open and drain black beans and corn and add to bowl. Add lime juice, olive oil, and salt and pepper to taste. Let salad stand for 15 minutes.

3. **Layer the salad.** On each of the serving plates, layer the following in order:
   ❖ Handfuls of chips to cover the bottom of each plate
   ❖ Spoonfuls of seasoned meat
   ❖ Spoonfuls of black bean and corn salad
   ❖ Grated sharp cheddar cheese
   ❖ Shredded Romaine lettuce
   ❖ Garnish of choice: fresh salsa, chopped cilantro, sour cream, and guacamole

Roasty Toasty Red Potato Salad

Regular old potato salads can't match this flavorful dish!

⏰ PLAN AHEAD!

The potatoes in this recipe roast for about an hour before making the salad. The flavors meld together best if you allow salad to sit for another hour before serving.

INGREDIENTS:

3 pounds small red potatoes, chunked

3 tablespoons olive oil

 ½ cup bacon bits

Salt and pepper, to taste

⅓ cup olive oil

Juice from 2 medium lemons

1 garlic clove, minced

1 bunch Italian flat leaf parsley, minced

1 bunch fresh chives, chopped

SERVES 8

TOOLS:

- Knife
- Cutting board
- Baking sheet with sides
- Measuring spoons & cups
- Small bowl
- Whisk

13

 1. Preheat oven to 400° F.

 2. Rinse off potatoes and dry them, but do not peel. Chunk potatoes into large pieces and toss on baking sheet with the 3 tablespoons of olive oil. Add salt and pepper to taste. Bake for about 1 hour until potatoes are browned and crispy.

3. Combine bacon bits, the $\frac{1}{3}$ cup of olive oil, fresh lemon juice, minced garlic, parsley, and chives in a small bowl and whisk together well. Pour this dressing over hot potatoes. Allow salad to sit for at least an hour before serving to let flavors blend together. Serve at room temperature.

Happy Face Soup

Sour cream makes the face but our creamy tomato soup will make *you* smile!

INGREDIENTS:

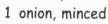

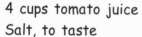

2 tablespoons butter
1 onion, minced
2 tablespoons flour
4 cups tomato juice
Salt, to taste
2 cups milk
1 small container sour cream

TOOLS:

- Knife
- Cutting board
- Soup pot
- Measuring cups and spoons
- Whisk
- Plastic sandwich bag
- Scissors

STEPS:

1. Heat soup pot over medium heat and add butter until melted. Add minced onions and sauté until translucent (almost see-through), about 5 minutes. Remove from heat and stir in flour with a whisk until there are no more lumps.

2. Put pot back on stove and turn heat on. Slowly whisk in tomato juice and salt to taste. Cook until just boiling. Turn off heat when it boils. Let cool for 10 minutes then slowly whisk in milk.

3. Put some sour cream in a plastic sandwich bag. Cut a tiny hole in the corner and squeeze the sour cream out to make your happy face! Serve immediately.

Friendship Soup

In the classic folktale "Stone Soup", a soup made from stones and water becomes a grand feast for a whole village. Ask each guest or classmate to bring one of the ingredients from each list below and you will make your own grand feast!

TOOLS:

◆ Soup pot
◆ Soup ladle
◆ Bowls

INGREDIENTS FOR YOU TO PROVIDE:

4 14.5-ounce cans of chicken, beef or vegetable broth

Salt & pepper

INGREDIENTS FOR GUESTS TO BRING:

List 1:

½ potato, peeled and chunked

1 carrot, peeled and sliced

1 broccoli stalk, chunked

½ turnip, peeled and chunked

1 stalk celery, sliced

6 green beans, chunked

Ingredients For Guests To Bring:

List 2:

- 1 cup corn kernels
- 1 cup frozen green peas, thawed
- ½ cup red/green cabbage, shredded

- 2 stalks green onion, sliced
- 10 spinach leaves, shredded
- ½ red pepper, seeded and diced

Steps:

1. Sort the vegetables into 2 piles. Place all the List 1 items in one pile and all the List 2 items in another.

2. Put the soup broth into the large soup pot. Add the vegetables from List 1. Turn the stove to high and bring soup to a boil. Reduce heat to medium and let soup simmer for 10 minutes.

3. Add the vegetables from List 2 and let the soup simmer for 15 more minutes. Add salt and pepper to taste. Be careful when tasting the spiciness and saltiness of the soup as the liquid is hot.

Enjoy this healthy soup with your best friends or classmates!

Chicken Noodle Doodle Soup

We hope you get all warm and fuzzy inside when you eat this all-time favorite.

INGREDIENTS:

- 1 pound boneless, skinless chicken meat
- 4 cubes chicken-flavored bouillon
- 8 cups water
- 1 carrot, peeled and diced
- ½ cup frozen peas
- 1 pound fun shaped pasta*

TOOLS:
- ◆ Soup pot
- ◆ Slotted spoon

*Use little chicken shapes, soccer balls, or any fun shape, all found readily available at grocery stores.

STEPS:

1. In a large pot, add chicken, bouillon, and water. Bring to a boil and then turn down the heat to simmer. Continue cooking until chicken is fully cooked and meat is no longer pink inside (about 25-30 minutes).

2. Remove chicken from broth with slotted spoon. Chop into small pieces and return meat to pot.

3. Add carrots, peas, and pasta shapes and cook pasta until tender.

ADD SOME CRUNCHIES TO YOUR SOUP:

- ❖ Popcorn, flavored
- ❖ Old fashioned oyster soup-crackers
- ❖ Bagel chips
- ❖ Crushed tortilla chips
- ❖ Small round pretzels
- ❖ Bacon bits
- ❖ Goldfish crackers
- ❖ Freshly baked croutons

Saté on a Stick

SERVES 6

PLAN AHEAD!

The skewers need to marinate for about an hour before grilling.

INGREDIENTS:

- 1 pound thinly sliced steak like flank or beef round
- 1 pound thinly sliced boneless chicken breast
- ½ cup vegetable oil
- ½ cup brown sugar
- ¾ cup soy sauce
- 3 cloves garlic, minced
- 1 cup pineapple juice or ½ cup crushed pineapple

TOOLS:

- ◆ Knife
- ◆ Cutting board
- ◆ Wood skewers
- ◆ 9 x 13-inch baking pan
- ◆ Measuring cups
- ◆ Mixing bowl
- ◆ Whisk
- ◆ Foil
- ◆ Metal BBQ tongs

STEPS:

1. Slice steak and chicken into long, thin strips. Thread each strip separately on a wooden skewer and put them into the baking pan.

2. Whisk together oil, brown sugar, soy sauce, garlic, and pineapple in a bowl. Pour over the skewers in the baking pan, cover with foil, and put in the refrigerator to marinate for at least an hour. The longer they marinate, the more flavorful they will be.

3. Have an adult BBQ the skewers, turning several times with metal tongs until lightly brown on all sides. Note that these cook fast! Serve with white rice for a tasty lunch.

Spice up your lunch with our "fowl" finger food!

⏰ PLAN AHEAD!

The wings need to marinate for at least 4 hours (best overnight) before baking!

INGREDIENTS:

24 chicken wing drummettes

½ cup hot pepper sauce of choice*

1 teaspoon garlic salt

2 tablespoons butter

1 cup dry biscuit mix

½ teaspoon onion salt

½ teaspoon ground black pepper

¼ teaspoon cayenne pepper

*There are many varieties of hot pepper sauces at the grocery store. Choose one that is not too hot for your taste buds to handle!

SERVES 4

TOOLS:

- ◆ 2 large zipper lock plastic bags
- ◆ Measuring cups & spoons
- ◆ Baking sheet, greased

Steps:

1. In a zipper lock plastic bag combine chicken drummettes with hot sauce and garlic salt. Let marinate in refrigerator for at least 4 hours (best overnight).

2. Preheat oven to 400° F.

3. In second zipper lock plastic bag combine biscuit mix, butter, onion salt, black and cayenne pepper. Add marinated drummettes to baking mix and coat, then place on prepared baking sheet. Bake for 25 minutes or until middle is no longer pink.

Sweet Honey-Mustard Dip

Dip your wings into this sweet dip or use a store bought Ranch dressing.

- ❖ ½ cup sour cream
- ❖ 3 tablespoons honey
- ❖ 3 tablespoons Dijon-style mustard

Serve this warm or chilled as a dip for wings.

Cowboy Willy's Chili

Make with cornbread on a snow day or on one of those really cold afternoons when you need to stay inside.

SERVES
4

INGREDIENTS:

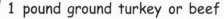

1 pound ground turkey or beef
1 medium onion, chopped
1 green bell pepper, chopped
1 teaspoon garlic powder
2 teaspoons chili powder
$\frac{1}{8}$ teaspoon cayenne pepper
1 teaspoon salt
1 14.5-ounce can diced tomatoes
1 6-ounce can tomato paste
1 cup water
1 can kidney beans, drained
1 package cornbread mix from grocery store
Grated cheddar cheese

STEPS:

TOOLS:
- Soup pot or skillet
- Large spoon
- Colander
- Measuring spoons
- Spatula
- Spoon
- Cutting board & chopping knife
- Can opener
- Ladle
- Grater

 1. Heat the soup pot or skillet over medium-high heat and add the meat, breaking it up and stirring until browned. Drain meat in colander.

 2. Put drained meat back in the pot over medium-high heat. Add the onion, green bell pepper, garlic, chili powder, cayenne pepper, and salt. Cook until soft, while stirring, about 4 minutes.

 3. Now, add diced tomatoes, tomato paste, and water to the pot. Stir well and bring to a boil. Then add the drained can of kidney beans. Lower heat to low and simmer for 30 minutes, uncovered, stirring occasionally.

4. While your chili is simmering, make the cornbread according to the directions on the package. (Check the box for any extra ingredients you might need.)

 5. Remove chili from heat and ladle chili into bowls. Serve with grated cheddar cheese on top and cornbread. Cozy!

Sloppy Turkey Joes

Poor Joe got blamed for this messy (but tasty) dish that tends to drip off the roll and plate and onto your lap. Be sure to tuck a napkin in your collar before eating so we can change the name to *Neat* Turkey Joes.

Ingredients:

- 2 tablespoons vegetable oil
- 1 large onion, diced
- 1 red bell pepper, seeded and diced
- 2 cloves garlic, minced
- 1 teaspoon dried oregano leaves
- 2 pounds lean ground turkey
- 3 6-ounce cans tomato paste
- 3 tablespoons sugar
- 3 tablespoons Worcestershire sauce
- 2 tablespoons red wine vinegar
- $\frac{1}{2}$ cup water
- $\frac{1}{2}$ teaspoon salt
- $\frac{1}{2}$ teaspoon black pepper
- 6 hamburger buns

Steps:

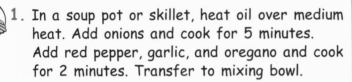

1. In a soup pot or skillet, heat oil over medium heat. Add onions and cook for 5 minutes. Add red pepper, garlic, and oregano and cook for 2 minutes. Transfer to mixing bowl.

2. Re-heat pot over medium-high heat and stir in turkey, breaking it up as it cooks. Cook until lightly browned, about 5 minutes.

3. Stir in vegetables from step 1, tomato paste, sugar, Worcestershire sauce, vinegar, water, salt and pepper. Bring the mixture to a simmer, then cover and cook for 20 minutes.

4. Lightly toast buns and place each one on a separate plate. Spoon a large scoop of Sloppy Joes on each one.

Yummy and Messy!

Tools:

- ◆ Soup pot or skillet
- ◆ Measuring spoons & cups
- ◆ Knife
- ◆ Cutting board
- ◆ Mixing bowl

The All American Hot Dog

Everyone loves hot dogs! Here are some favorite ways to enjoy them.

Ways To Eat Them:

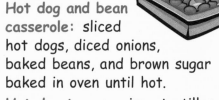

Panini or grilled: slice hot dogs open, grill the inside and put between toasted, sliced roll with melted cheese.

Hot dog fondue: dip hot dog slices into melted cheese sauce.

Hot dog pizza: use sliced hot dogs instead of pepperoni.

Hot dog and bean casserole: sliced hot dogs, diced onions, baked beans, and brown sugar baked in oven until hot.

Hot dog tacos: crispy tortillas with long hot dog slices, shredded lettuce, grated cheese, and salsa.

Hot dogs in a blanket: hot dog baked in biscuit from refrigerated roll.

Hot dog ciabatta club: ciabatta is a big roll layered up with a hot dog and other deli goodies to make a "hot dog club".

Dodger dog: found only in Los Angeles, California, at the top baseball park in the US. The most hot dogs served —over 1.6 million in 2004!

Stuffed hot dog: slice down the middle, stuff with cheese, sauerkraut, chili, or any filling of choice!

Hot dog kebabs: alternate thick slices of hot dog with onion, bell pepper, mini potatoes, and other veggies on wooden skewers.

Hot Doggie-O's: cook small slices with a favorite pasta and sauce.

Hot Dog Soup: put several hot dogs in a blender and puree. Heat in microwave safe bowl and serve with ketchup on top.

Twice As Nice Potatoes

Everyone loves potatoes and here's a recipe that makes them doubly good!

INGREDIENTS:

- 4 large russet potatoes
- 4 tablespoons butter, melted
- 2 tablespoons sour cream
- 2 tablespoons bacon bits
- ½ cup green onion, diced
- 2 cups fresh spinach, washed and shredded
- 2 cups cheddar cheese, grated

TOOLS:

- Sponge
- Knife
- Cutting board
- Baking sheet
- Fork
- Melon baller or small spoon
- Mixing bowl
- Measuring spoons & cups
- Large spoon

STEPS:

1. Preheat oven to 450° F.

2. Wash and scrub the outside of the potato skins with a clean sponge and pat dry. Cut each one in half and put on a baking sheet with the skin side down. Bake for 15-20 minutes until soft and able to prick with a fork. Take out of oven and let sit for 5 minutes.

3. Scoop out the insides of each potato half and put into a mixing bowl. Add melted butter, sour cream, bacon bits, diced green onion, and spinach. Mix together well.

4. Generously scoop the potato mixture back into each of the potato skins and sprinkle $\frac{1}{4}$ cup of the grated cheese on top of each one. Reduce heat on oven to 350° and bake until heated through, about 20 minutes. Dig in!

Wrap & Roll Lunchbox

Let's go wrap and roll! There are so many fun ways to make these sandwiches and once you do, wrap them tightly in foil and they make a perfect lunchbox treat.

WRAP OPTIONS:

Tortillas
flour, white corn, or use some of the many-colored and flavored ones available

Lavash flat bread

Pita bread
cut in half

Lettuce leaves
butter lettuce or Romaine works best, washed and dried

Cabbage leaves
red or purple leaves are fun, washed and dried

Wonton wrappers
for mini wraps

FILLING OPTIONS:

❖ Cooked and shredded beef, chicken or pork, mixed with favorite barbeque sauce

❖ Black beans, corn kernels, chopped cilantro, and salsa

❖ Ham, cheese, and finely chopped fresh pineapple

❖ Turkey, Swiss cheese, and avocado slices

❖ Softened cream cheese with chopped salami, tomatoes, and fresh basil

* Peanut butter, banana, and mini chocolate chips

* Softened cream cheese and jam preserves of choice

* Egg salad topped with celery slices

* Apple slices drizzled with maple syrup and cinnamon sugar sprinkles

* Cooked egg noodles, thin slices of chicken, shredded carrots drizzled with Asian sesame dressing

EASY TO MAKE:

1. Choose a wrapper and place on slightly larger piece of foil.

2. Choose a filling. If chunky, use about ½ cup and spread evenly in the middle of wrapper. If creamy, spread a thin layer or layers evenly over the wrapper. If deli style, make thin layers of lunchmeats and cheese.

3. Use the foil to tightly wrap into a vertical roll. Tuck the edges of the short sides of the roll under so you can peel open the top of the foil when ready to eat. Just keep peeling the foil down as you go, so none of the goodies fall out.

We're Talking Turkey Salad Pita

Scoop this salad into a pita and you have a tasty sandwich pocket for school.

INGREDIENTS:

- 1 pound smoked turkey breast, chunked
- ½ pound red seedless grapes, removed from stem
- ½ large cantaloupe, seeded and chunked
- 4 green onions, sliced
- 2 celery stalks, sliced
- ½ cup golden raisins
- ¾ cup sliced almonds
- ⅓ cup mayonnaise
- ¼ cup plain yogurt
- ¼ cup sour cream
- 2 teaspoons curry powder
- Pita bread

SERVES 6

TOOLS:

- ◆ Knife
- ◆ Cutting board
- ◆ Large mixing bowl
- ◆ Large spoon
- ◆ Small mixing bowl
- ◆ Measuring cups & spoons
- ◆ Whisk

STEPS:

1. Prepare turkey, grapes, cantaloupe, green onions, and celery as described in ingredient list and put in large bowl.

2. Add raisins and almonds and mix together.

3. In the small bowl, whisk together mayonnaise, yogurt, sour cream, and curry powder to make dressing.

4. Toss this dressing with turkey and fruit and scoop into pita halves.

Sweet Meatball Sandwiches

MAKES 4 SANDWICHES

The goodies in the sauce make these so delightfully sweet!

INGREDIENTS:

- 1 jar of grape jelly (not jam)
- 1 bottle of chili sauce
- ¼ cup brown sugar
- 16 cooked meatballs—use frozen and thawed pre-made ones or make your own
- 4 French rolls
- Parmesan cheese, grated
- Shredded lettuce

STEPS:

1. Mix together grape jelly, chili sauce, and brown sugar in pot over low heat. Add meatballs and stir occasionally. Let meatballs simmer in sauce for 20 minutes.

2. Slice open each French roll and put 4 meatballs inside. Spoon some of the extra sweet sauce on top, then some parmesan cheese and shredded lettuce. If you wrap these up tightly in foil, they are great for the lunchbox.

TOOLS:

- Soup pot
- Measuring cup
- Spoon
- Knife

A Tuna Fishy

Cut bread into fun fish shapes and this sandwich will swim right into your stomach!

TOOLS:
- Can opener
- Mixing bowl
- Measuring spoons
- Knife
- Cutting board
- Spoon

MAKES 2 CUPS OF TUNA

INGREDIENTS:

One 12-ounce can of water-packed tuna

2 tablespoons mayonnaise

2 tablespoons Ranch dressing

1 celery stalk, diced

Handful of Spanish olives, diced

Salt and pepper, to taste

Large sourdough bread slices

STEPS:

1. Open the tuna, drain out the water, and put in mixing bowl. Add mayonnaise, Ranch dressing, diced celery, and Spanish olives and mix together well. Add salt and pepper to taste.

2. Layer two bread slices on top of each other and cut into a fish shape. Spread tuna between bread and add a sliced Spanish olive eye.

BLT, PBJ, Etc.

Here are two short-cut names for a couple of all-time favorite sandwiches.

BLT (Bacon, Lettuce, and Tomato)

Tools:
- Heavy skillet
- Metal tongs
- Paper towels
- Butter knife
- Sharp knife
- Cutting board

Ingredients:

- 12 slices bacon
- 8 slices white bread
- Mayonnaise
- 2 medium tomatoes, sliced
- Salt
- 4 iceberg lettuce leaves

SERVES 4

Steps:

1. Heat skillet to medium or medium-low. Lay slices of bacon flat in skillet and cook slowly, turning often with metal tongs until crisp to liking. Place cooked bacon strips on paper towels to drain off excess fat.

2. Toast the bread slices and spread mayonnaise on each slice.

3. Pile tomato slices on 4 slices of bread and sprinkle with a little salt. Top with bacon, lettuce, and second slice of bread. Slice sandwiches in half. Enjoy this sandwich while it is still warm.

PBJ (Peanut Butter and Jelly) 🥜●○

OK, so we can't make this one too easy. You need to make your own chunky PB first!

Ingredients:

- Two ¼-cup roasted, unsalted, shelled peanuts
- 5 tablespoons canola or peanut oil
- 2 teaspoons salt
- Favorite bread
- Favorite jelly or jam

Optional Toppings:

Raisins, craisins, banana chips or other dried fruits, granola, sunflower seeds, cashews, sliced bananas, apples, or strawberries, drizzle of maple syrup or honey

Tools:

- ◆ Food processor
- ◆ Measuring cups
- ◆ Small bowl
- ◆ Butter knife

MAKES ABOUT 1½ CUPS

Steps:

1. Add peanuts to food processor and pulse just 4 times. Scoop out ¼ cup of chopped peanuts and put in small bowl. Add oil and salt to peanuts in food processor and process for 15 minutes or until creamy, turning machine on and off every few minutes to scrape down sides. Stir in chopped peanuts to make it crunchy.

2. Spread on bread with jam or jelly. Save remaining PB in covered bowl in refrigerator.

Light and Dark Canapés

A canapé is a small, thin piece of bread spread with cheese, meats, or any favorite filling. Make them two-tone by using light and dark-colored mini breads.

Ingredients:

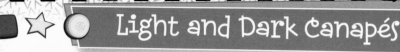

2 cucumbers, sliced

1 loaf cocktail size white or sourdough bread (light)

1 loaf cocktail size wheat or pumpernickel bread (dark)

1 container whipped cream cheese

Tools:

- Large cutting board
- Paring knife
- Butter knife
- Small cookie cutters in fun shapes

STEPS:

1. Thinly slice cucumbers in about $\frac{1}{8}$-inch-wide slices.

2. Place the white bread slices in pairs on a cutting board. Lightly spread cream cheese on the top pieces. Then place one thin slice of cucumber on top of the cream cheese and top with the remaining bread slices. Repeat this process with the dark bread.

3. Using the cookie cutters, press out the middles of the sandwiches and take them out. Place the white cut-out in the dark frame and the dark cut-out in the white frames to create a two-toned looked. You can also just serve the cut-outs or just the frames to make it all fun.

OTHER FUN FILLINGS:

❖ Ricotta cheese and strawberry jam

❖ Ham and Swiss cheese

❖ Bologna and American cheese

❖ Hazelnut chocolate spread and raspberry preserves

❖ Egg Salad

❖ Smoked salmon and thin sliced red onion

The Night Before Stuffed Sandwiches

Every lunch needs sandwiches and these are extra special and easy to make. Buy any type of fresh bakery rolls that have a hard crusty outside like a French baguette, Kaiser roll, or submarine roll. Halve lengthwise and pull out most of the bread inside. Fill with one of the sandwich stuffing ideas listed on page 44 that is moist but not too wet. Wrap tightly in plastic wrap and chill overnight. Not only do you avoid the rush of making sandwiches in the morning, but also the filling flavors meld together delightfully!

⏰ PLAN AHEAD!

These sandwiches are best when they set overnight.

Sandwich Stuffing Ideas

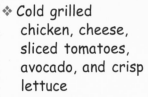

❖ Cold grilled chicken, cheese, sliced tomatoes, avocado, and crisp lettuce

❖ Tuna salad with celery, mayonnaise, a little yogurt, and some green onion tops

❖ Jack cheese, cream cheese, a splash of fresh salsa, chopped cilantro, and crisp lettuce

❖ Sliced provolone, salami, tomatoes, lettuce, and Italian salad dressing

❖ Turkey breast, Swiss cheese, fresh spinach leaves, and a touch of ranch dressing

❖ Cream cheese, carrots, lettuce, tomato, sprouts, and peanuts

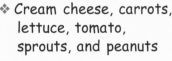

❖ Chicken salad with mayonnaise, celery, onion, diced apple, and dill

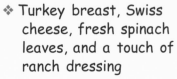

❖ Cold thinly sliced steak with Swiss cheese, lettuce, and spicy mustard

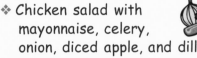

❖ Diced chicken, stir fried vegetables with soy sauce, fresh ginger, and sesame seeds

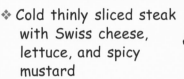

The Race Car Sandwich

You'll race to make this sandwich that looks like a racecar! Zoom! Watch it go!

INGREDIENTS:

Fresh soft roll or torpedo roll, cut open

Cucumber slice for windshield

Cherry tomato for driver's head

Salami and carrot slices for wheels

Carrot slices or grape halves for headlights

Mayonnaise

Favorite sandwich filling

TOOLS:

- Knife
- Cutting board
- Toothpicks
- Plastic sandwich bag
- Spoon
- Twist tie or rubber band
- Scissors

STEPS:

1. Split and fill sandwich, being careful to keep filling inside roll.

2. Cut a cucumber slice in half. Make a slice in the front $\frac{1}{3}$ of the roll and insert the half cucumber as a windshield.

3. Insert a toothpick into a cherry tomato and stick it behind windshield for the driver's head.

4. Make colorful wheels out of salami and carrot slices strung on toothpicks. Stick four wheels on the car. Insert toothpicks in carrot slices on the front for headlights.

5. Spoon some mayonnaise into one corner of a small sandwich bag. Put a twist tie or rubber band on top and cut a tiny hole in the corner. You now have a decorating bag!

6. Use your decorating bag to draw car details like a front grill, doors, racing stripes, and car numbers. Be sure to make a silly face on the driver. Add a small flag and you're ready to go!

Be careful to take out toothpicks before eating. ZOOM!

Nosh & Nibbles

ALL RECIPES MAKE ABOUT 20 SNACK SIZE SERVINGS

Every lunch needs some good snacks. Here are several ways to make a good old favorite.

CHEX MIX! TRADITIONAL

6 tablespoon butter, melted

1 teaspoon seasoned salt

4 teaspoons Worcestershire sauce

2 cups Rice Chex Cereal

2 cups Corn Chex Cereal

2 cups Wheat Chex Cereal

$\frac{3}{4}$ cups salted mixed nuts

Preheat oven to 250° F. Put melted butter in a 13 x 9-inch baking pan and stir in seasoned salt and Worcestershire sauce. Mix in Chex cereals and nuts and put in oven 45 minutes. Stir every 15 minutes. Spread on paper towel to cool.

(See page 48 for tools you will need.)

Minty Marshmallow

6 cups popped popcorn

4 cups Corn or Rice Chex Cereal

7 ounce jar marshmallow cream

20 red or green hard peppermint candies, coarsely crushed, about ½ cup

Tools:
- 13 x 9-inch baking dish
- Large spoon
- Paper towel
- Wax paper

Preheat oven to 350° F. Mix together popcorn and Chex on greased baking sheet. Microwave marshmallow cream for 1-2 minutes until soft and melted, then pour over popcorn mixture and stir until evenly coated. Sprinkle with crushed mint candies and bake for 5 minutes or longer until coating is light golden brown. Spread on wax paper to cool. Break into pieces.

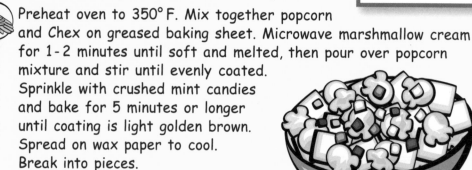

White Chocolate

1 pound white chocolate, melted
3 cups Rice Chex Cereal
3 cups Corn Chex Cereal
3 cups Cheerios
3 cups pretzels
2 cups mixed nuts
12 ounces plain M&M's

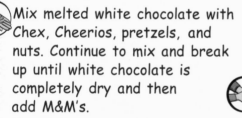

Mix melted white chocolate with Chex, Cheerios, pretzels, and nuts. Continue to mix and break up until white chocolate is completely dry and then add M&M's.

Optional items: add chocolate chips, chocolate covered raisins, and peanut butter pieces

Chunky Funky

1 cup butter, melted
1 cup light corn syrup
1 cup sugar
6 cups Rice Chex Cereal
6 cup honey grahams
1 cup slivered almonds
1 cup cashew halves
1 cup shredded sweetened coconut flakes

Melt butter with corn syrup and sugar. Mix with Chex, grahams, almonds, cashews, and coconut. Spread on wax paper and cool. Break up into pieces.

The Blue Lagoon

MAKES 1 LARGE JELL-O SALAD

Jell-O has never been so much fun as this fishy blue salad!

⏰ PLAN AHEAD!

Like all Jell-O, it needs to refrigerate for at least 4 hours. Best to make in the evening and let set completely overnight.

TOOLS:

◆ Measuring cups
◆ Large glass bowl
◆ Large spoon

INGREDIENTS:

Two 6-ounce boxes of blue Jell-O
1 pint of fresh blueberries, washed
Gummy fish, sharks, octopus,
   or combination of all

STEPS:

1. Make both boxes of Jell-O in large glass bowl according to the instructions on the box. Drop the blueberries in so they float around like bubbles. Put the Jell-O in the refrigerator and let it slightly set for about 1-2 hours.

2. Take Jell-O out and press the gummy sea life all around inside the big blue lagoon. Put back into the refrigerator and let it set completely. The recommended total time needed is 4 hours; but sometimes with a glass bowl, it may take a bit longer.

Popsicles, Popsicles & Plenty More!

You are sure to find a flavor here that you like!

Watermelon Popsicles

1 cup seedless watermelon chunks
1 cup orange juice
1 cup water

Put watermelon, orange juice, and water in blender and puree. Pour into molds and freeze.

Raspberry Tangerine Popsicles

1 pint fresh whole raspberries
2 cups tangerine juice

Divide raspberries among Popsicle molds. Pour in juice and freeze.

Rocky Road Popsicles

1 package chocolate pudding mix
½ cup miniature marshmallows
¼ cup chopped walnuts

Make pudding according to package instructions. Stir in marshmallows and walnuts. Scoop into Popsicle molds and freeze.

Tools:

◆ Measuring cup
◆ Blender
◆ Popsicle molds

CREAMY POPSICLES

6-ounce can frozen orange juice concentrate, softened (or grape juice, cranberry, or lemonade)

6 ounces water

1 pint vanilla ice cream or plain frozen yogurt, softened

Put juice concentrate, water and ice cream in blender and puree. Pour into molds and freeze.

PEACHY KEEN POPSICLES

2 fresh ripe peaches, sliced and pitted or one 8-ounce can peaches in light syrup, drained

1 cup heavy cream

1 teaspoon honey

Put peaches, cream, and honey in blender and puree. Pour into molds and freeze.

Make Popsicles with any of these fun and delicious juices:

- ❖ Orange
- ❖ Tangerine
- ❖ Apple
- ❖ Grape
- ❖ Cranberry
- ❖ Carrot
- ❖ Lemonade
- ❖ Mango
- ❖ Passion fruit
- ❖ Strawberry-kiwi
- ❖ Cherry
- ❖ Pineapple

Cheesy Baked Raspberry

Part cheese, part fruit, and part chocolate—a terrific tasting trio!

Ingredients:

3 eggs

One 15-ounce container of ricotta cheese

½ cup honey

1 cup frozen raspberries, thawed

2 tablespoons sugar

Fresh raspberries and chocolate sauce for garnish

Tools:

- ◆ Medium mixing bowl
- ◆ Whisk
- ◆ Large spoon
- ◆ Measuring cups & spoons
- ◆ 4 heatproof custard cups, greased
- ◆ Blender

STEPS:

1. Preheat oven to 350°F.

2. Separate egg yolks from whites. Discard yolks and save whites in a mixing bowl. Whisk whites until foamy.

3. Stir in ricotta cheese and honey and mix together well. Spoon batter into greased custard cups. Bake for 35 minutes or until cakes are light golden.

4. Put thawed raspberries and sugar into a blender and puree until sauce is almost smooth.

5. Pour sauce over warm cakes. Garnish with fresh raspberries and drizzle with chocolate sauce. Delicious!

THE LUNCH KITCHEN IS CLOSED

However, it's not closed for long, because there is always another lunch to pack, midday meal to enjoy with friends, or recipe that you haven't yet tried. So let's do lunch again! We hope this cookbook helped you:

◆ Make new friends (Friendship Soup),

◆ Learn that lunch can be fishy (The Blue Lagoon or A Tuna Fishy),

◆ And lunch can be messy (Sloppy Turkey Joes) but for now, we will just

◆ Wrap things up (Wrap and Roll Lunchbox)!

Be responsible and take care of the cooking kit you received this month by hand washing and drying utensils after each use.

More fabulous cookbooks are coming from Kids Cooking Club soon. We look forward to sharing our love of cooking with you some more!

www.kidscook.com